THE NEW BOOK OF

PHARAOHS

Dr Anne Millard

ALADDIN/WATTS
LONDON • SYDNEY

Contents

© Aladdin Books Ltd
1998
*Designed and
produced by*
Aladdin Books Ltd
28 Percy Street
London W1P 0LD

ISBN 0 7496 3178 3

*First published in Great
Britain in 1998 by*
Aladdin/Watts Books
96 Leonard Street
London EC2A 4RH
Printed in Belgium
All rights reserved

Editor
Jon Richards
Design

David West
CHILDREN'S BOOK DESIGN

Designer
Flick Killerby
Illustrators
Richard Rockwood
& Rob Shone

Picture Research
Brooks Krikler Research

A CIP catalogue entry for this
book is available from the
British Library.

The author, Dr Anne Millard, has worked on digs for
the Egypt Exploration Society, lectures for the
Extramural Department of London University and has
written numerous books on history and archaeology.

INTRODUCTION

Around the time of 3100 BC, the kingdom of
Egypt was united by King Menes. This
started the growth of one of the greatest
nations ever seen. Over the next 3,000 years,
Egypt was to grow, at one time creating an
empire which stretched from Nubia in the
south to Palestine in the north. Throughout
this land the ancient Egyptians built huge
monuments to house their dead and to
worship their gods, goddesses and ancestors.
Many of these monuments now lie in ruins,
or are hidden completely from view. It is the
job of the archaeologist to find these
buildings and try to piece them back
together so that we can recreate
what life may have been like
in ancient Egypt.

Despite the development of modern technology which allows today's Egyptologists to study monuments and remains in more detail than ever before, there is still no substitute for archaeologists painstakingly sifting through the shattered and hidden remains. This book examines some of the most recent finds, revealing the latest discoveries as they are unearthed.

Today, archaeologists can use modern technology to help them study the remains of the Egyptian kingdom. *The New Book of Pharaohs* will show some of these modern techniques. These include the use of x-rays and CAT scans, which can peer inside mummies and coffins without having to open them up and damage them, and the use of cameras with air-locks, which can look inside tombs without exposing them to the outside air. They have also developed computer programmes which, if enough information is fed into them, can recreate just how a monument might have looked in its heyday.

ANCIENT EGYPT

The history of ancient Egypt can be divided into several periods. First came the Archaic Period (c.3100–2650 BC) and this was followed by the period known as the Old Kingdom (c.2650–2134 BC). After this there was a brief break called the First Intermediate Period (c.2134–2040 BC), and then the Middle Kingdom (c.2040–1640 BC), the Second Intermediate Period (c.1640–1550 BC), the New Kingdom (c.1550–1070 BC), the Third Intermediate Period (c.1070–712 BC), the Late Period (c.712–332 BC) and finally the Graeco-Roman Period (c.332 BC – 395 AD). During these periods, Egypt was ruled by various families, called dynasties. In total there were 32 dynasties, beginning with King Narmer of Dynasty I and ending with Cleopatra VII of the 32nd Dynasty.

CHAPTER ONE
THE LOST TOMB

The deserts of Egypt are rich with the remnants of the ancient kingdom that flourished for nearly 3,500 years. This chapter will show some of the latest archaeological discoveries, and some re-discoveries, from ancient tombs to lost cities.

Particularly rich in remains is the Valley of the Kings. Here, the Egyptians buried their New Kingdom rulers in underground tombs (*see* map below). One particular re-discovery, in 1987, involved the excavation of the tomb known as KV5. Archaeologists were amazed to discover that the tomb had been built for some of the many sons of the Pharaoh Ramesses II.

Guide to the Valley of the Kings

A Sons of Ramesses II	G Ramesses III
B Ramesses IX	H Ramesses V/VI
C Ramesses X	I Tutankhamun
D Sethos I	J Merenptah
E Ramesses I	K Ramesses II
F Amenmesse	

Valley of the Kings

The Valley of the Kings is situated on the West Bank of the Nile opposite the modern city of Luxor (*left*). Some 62 tombs have been discovered so far, including the famous tomb of Tutankhamun (*see* page 15).

Despite its name, the valley does not just include the tombs of kings. A few tombs have been found to contain the remains of favoured princes and nobles.

RAMESSES THE GREAT

Ramesses II, the Great, ruled Egypt between about 1304–1237 BC. He was a warrior king, who claimed great victories, and was a prolific builder (he built the enormous temples at Abu Simbel – *see* pages 18-19). He had several queens, numerous minor wives and about 200 children! He died an old man, and studies of his mummy (*right*) showed that he suffered from arthritis, heart disease and bad teeth.

The Valley of the Kings

When Kent Weeks opened the tomb KV5 in 1987, it was not for the first time. The tomb was first discovered in the early nineteenth century, but over the years floods had carried tonnes of sand and rocks into the tomb, filling it almost to the roof. People believed it was not worth clearing, the entrance was covered with sand and the tomb was lost.

KENT WEEKS

Working for the Cairo American University, Professor Kent Weeks (*below*) has been surveying the West Bank in order to produce a detailed map of the area. Although tomb KV5 was known about, its exact location remained a mystery. Professor Weeks concentrated his search near to the tomb of Ramesses IX. However, before he could start he had to persuade souvenir stall holders to move!

T-shaped corridor

Large pillared hall

Storage chambers

Descending corridor

Ramesses' own tomb, called KV7, is large, but not as large as the one he built his sons. In fact, KV5 is the largest tomb in the valley! Inside the tomb are two storage chambers, a large pillared hall and a long T-shaped corridor with rooms along either side (*above*). Where the corridor divides stands a fine statue of Osiris, the god of the dead (*left*). Two newly discovered descending corridors near the entrance seem to be heading in the direction of Ramesses' tomb across the valley floor. Were they intended to link the two tombs?

AVARIS, CAPITAL OF THE HYKSOS

By about 1650 BC, Egypt's great Middle Kingdom (Dynasties XI to XIII) had collapsed in chaos. Invaders, who we call Hyksos, had crossed the Eastern frontier. 'Hyksos' comes from two ancient Egyptian words meaning 'rulers of foreign hill countries'. Armed with a deadly new weapon – the horse-drawn chariot – they overwhelmed the stunned Egyptians and set up a new state in the Delta. They chose a city called Avaris as their capital.

Little was known of these foreign rulers, until an excavation under the control of archaeologist Manfred Bietak found the exact location of Avaris. This on-going expedition has also unearthed many surprising treasures which have revealed some astounding facts about the life of the Hyksos.

Avaris

There has been much discussion about the location of the Hyksos' capital. Bietak's expedition pinpointed the site to modern-day Tell el-Dab'a in the Nile Delta (*left*).

Wall paintings found at Avaris appear to show young men and women leaping between the horns of a charging bull (*right*). They amazed archaeologists because of their similarity to paintings found at the Palace at Knossos on the island of Crete. The Avaris paintings even appear to be older than those at Knossos. Manfred Bietak also found fragments of paintings, also in the Cretan style, showing plants, trees, acrobats and hunting scenes.

The paintings at Knossos and Avaris show what archaeologists believe was a bull-leaping ceremony. In it, young acrobats would grab the horns of a bull and somersault over its back (*left*). These acrobats were highly respected for this ritual which may have had some religious purpose.

Cretan bull-leaping ceremony

Discoveries at Avaris have shown how well fortified it was. There were massive walls, 8.5 m (28 ft) thick at the base, and a heavily fortified fortress. After the Hyksos had left, the Egyptians demolished their fortress and built their own which was just as formidable (*left*).

DONKEY BURIALS

Bietak's dig has shown that Avaris was the centre of trade with Canaan, Syria and Crete and many of its inhabitants were Canaanites. Some Canaanites were traders and some graves at Avaris have a pair of donkeys sacrificed at the entrance (*below*) – not an Egyptian custom. Perhaps these men ran the donkey caravans that carried goods to Avaris.

Human skeleton

Donkey skeletons

THE CRETAN CONNECTION

Lying to the north of Egypt, the island of Crete saw the flowering of the Minoan civilisation between 1900 and 1400 BC. The huge palace at Knossos, whose remains can still be seen (*left*), was built around a central courtyard where the bull-leaping ceremony took place. Archaeologists are puzzled about the link between this distant civilisation and Egypt. It may be that a Cretan princess married a Hyksos or Egyptian king, who then decorated his palace to remind her of home.

FEUDING FAMILIES

The rulers of ancient Egypt were not without their intrigues or jealous arguments. One such incident involves the New Kingdom Pharaoh Tuthmosis III and his attempts to outshine his step-mother, Hatshepsut. Over the past 30 years, archaeologists have been discovering remains which indicate the lengths that Tuthmosis III went to in order to better Hatshepsut.

The family tree (*below*) shows how Tuthmosis III was Tuthmosis II's son by his marriage to one of his other wives, Isis. After Tuthmosis II's death, Tuthmosis III came to the throne with Hatshepsut acting as regent. However, in a brilliant coup, Hatshepsut replaced Tuthmosis III as outright ruler, humiliating the young king. After her death, Tuthmosis III set about getting his revenge by defacing her monuments and building his own in order to overshadow hers.

Many aspects of the reign of Queen Hatshepsut (*right*) remained a mystery until the work of Egyptian archaeologist Labib Habachi. He set about piecing together the smashed inscriptions on her monuments and looking at texts from private tombs that date from her reign. The picture that emerged was of a strong ruler who reigned for 20 years and a powerful warrior who led her troops into battle many times.

WILFUL DESTRUCTION

After Hatshepsut's death, Tuthmosis III gave orders to remove all traces of her existence. Her name was cut from her monuments, her pictures chiselled out (*below*) and her statues and inscriptions smashed. The walls of her funeral temple at Deir el Bahari (*see* right) were subject to particular violence. The work of Labib Habachi has shown that these inscriptions portrayed Hatshepsut's achievements, which included her own military victories. In a jealous rage, Tuthmosis III had these records destroyed so that they did not overshadow his own conquests.

KINGS OF DYNASTIES
XVII AND XVIII

= married

SENISENEB

AHMOSE = TUTHMOSIS I = MUTNOFRET

HATSHEPSUT = TUTHMOSIS II = ISIS

NEFERURE   MERYETRE HATSHEPSUT = TUTHMOSIS III

KEY

| KING | MALE CHILD | QUEEN | FEMALE CHILD |

PRIDE BEFORE THE FALL

Though smaller than Hatshepsut's funeral temple (*right*), Tuthmosis' temple was similar in design, but it was built at a higher level in order to overshadow his step-mother's monument (*below*). However, an earth slide later destroyed his temple, but left hers undamaged.

Temple of Tuthmosis III   *Temple of Hatshepsut*

Temple of Mentuhotep

Chapel of the goddess Hathor

THE LOST TEMPLE

In the 1960s, a team of Polish archaeologists began restoring the funeral temple of Hatshepsut. They started finding blocks from another temple, now totally destroyed, that had belonged to King Tuthmosis III (*right*). He had built a shrine to the god Amun next to Hatshepsut's funeral temple. All that remains now are broken fragments (*left*), which thousands of tourists ignore as they marvel at the beauty of Hatshepsut's temple!

ABYDOS, THE ROYAL CEMETERY

For many years, archaeologists have disagreed about the location of the final resting place of Egypt's earliest rulers, those from Dynasty I. At the turn of the century, the archaeologist Sir William Flinders Petrie found the remains of ten tombs at a site at Abydos in southern Egypt. The tomb stelae were marked with the names of Egypt's earliest kings, so it was assumed that the Dynasty I kings were buried in them. However, another archaeologist, Walter Emery, working at Sakkara in the 1930s and 1950s, found much larger tombs bearing the same Dynasty I names. He assumed that these were the resting places of the earliest kings. Most recently, an expedition in 1991 discovered boat burials and a series of even larger funeral monuments back at Abydos, indicating that the Dynasty I kings were, in fact, buried there.

Tomb stela

The 1991 expedition by Pennsylvania and Yale universities uncovered 12 wooden ships that were identical to those used during the Dynasty I period (*above*). They were 18–21 m (59–69 ft) long and had been placed in shallow trenches and covered in bricks. These boats, like those found by the Giza pyramids (*see* page 29), may have been intended to be used by the king during his afterlife.

THE AFTERLIFE

The Egyptians believed that, if they had led virtuous lives, they would be rewarded with eternal happiness. They also believed that they could provide for a comfortable eternity, by filling their tombs with their possessions and supplies. However, not all tombs contained actual replicas of possessions and servants. Many had to make do with models of their belongings (*right*).

Burial mounds for household servants

Situated on a wide desert plain some 145 km (90 miles) north of Luxor, the city of Abydos was sacred to the god of the dead, Osiris, and became one of the most holy places in early Egypt. The great temple, built there by Seti I, attracted pilgrims from all over the country.

Abydos

ABYDOS FUNERAL COMPLEXES

The tombs at Abydos (*below*) are smaller and less elaborate then those at Sakkara. They consist of a central tomb, which contained several rooms that were filled with offerings, and tomb stelae which contain the name of the buried king. Around some of the tombs are smaller subsidiary tombs. These held the bodies of what archaeologists believe were the kings' servants – one tomb had over 300 of these! New excavations have now revealed large mud-brick enclosures which were places where offerings were made to a king's spirit. These as well as the boats have confirmed Abydos to be the Dynasty I kings' final resting place.

Tomb stela

Main tomb

Subsidiary tombs

Storage rooms

It's easy to see why the tombs discovered by Walter Emery at Sakkara were mistaken for the graves of the Dynasty I kings. These rectangular, flat-topped tombs, called mastabas, were crammed full of treasure and provisions for the afterlife (*left*). They were also surrounded by the graves of courtiers and servants who had been sacrificed so that they could serve their lords and ladies after death. If, as archaeologists now believe, these tombs were not for the Dynasty I kings, then they must have belonged to important people, possibly members of the royal family or top officials.

Burial chamber

THE TOMBS OF SAKKARA

Even though archaeologists believe that it does not hold the bodies of Egypt's earliest kings, there is little doubt about Sakkara's importance as a cemetery – its position on the edge of the desert and its location near to the ancient capital of Memphis saw to that. Almost everybody was buried there, from later kings and queens, through great officials and the middle classes, right down to the humblest peasants. As well as the early mastaba tombs (*see* page 11), archaeologists have recently discovered the tombs of top-ranking officials from the reign of the boy-king, Tutankhamun, including his treasurer and one of his generals. They have also found a great number of mummified animals that were buried in underground galleries which riddle the ground beneath the area. These animal corpses were said to contain the spirits of gods and goddesses.

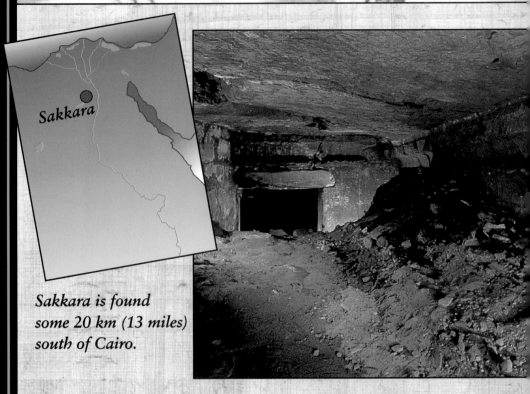

Sakkara is found some 20 km (13 miles) south of Cairo.

TOMB DECORATIONS

Once the insides of the tombs had been cleared of rubble (*above*) they revealed an unusual sight. Maya and his wife Merit had superb, golden-yellow paintings in theirs, while other tombs at Sakkara are not normally decorated.

ANIMAL MUMMIES

Once, whole species of animals were honoured as containers for the spirits of gods on Earth. Work at Sakkara by the Egypt Excavation Society (EES) has revealed that they embalmed and buried countless hawks, baboons, cats and ibises. The ibises were placed in huge underground galleries that run for great distances. The picture (*below*) shows Professor Emery of the EES entering one of these galleries.

A mummified baboon

Entrance to the animal galleries

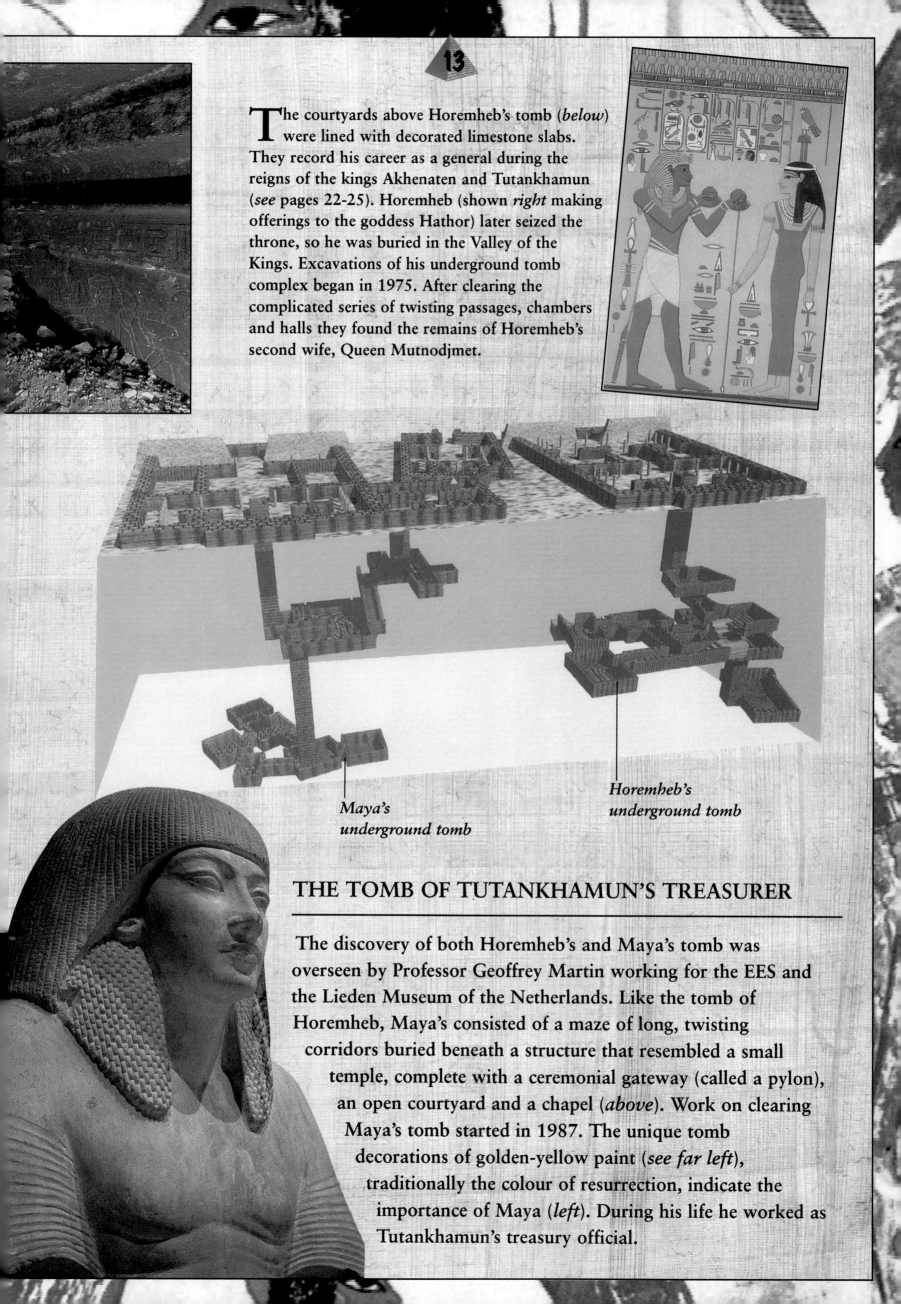

The courtyards above Horemheb's tomb (*below*) were lined with decorated limestone slabs. They record his career as a general during the reigns of the kings Akhenaten and Tutankhamun (*see* pages 22-25). Horemheb (shown *right* making offerings to the goddess Hathor) later seized the throne, so he was buried in the Valley of the Kings. Excavations of his underground tomb complex began in 1975. After clearing the complicated series of twisting passages, chambers and halls they found the remains of Horemheb's second wife, Queen Mutnodjmet.

Maya's underground tomb

Horemheb's underground tomb

THE TOMB OF TUTANKHAMUN'S TREASURER

The discovery of both Horemheb's and Maya's tomb was overseen by Professor Geoffrey Martin working for the EES and the Lieden Museum of the Netherlands. Like the tomb of Horemheb, Maya's consisted of a maze of long, twisting corridors buried beneath a structure that resembled a small temple, complete with a ceremonial gateway (called a pylon), an open courtyard and a chapel (*above*). Work on clearing Maya's tomb started in 1987. The unique tomb decorations of golden-yellow paint (*see far left*), traditionally the colour of resurrection, indicate the importance of Maya (*left*). During his life he worked as Tutankhamun's treasury official.

CHAPTER TWO
FINDING PHARAOHS

This chapter will look at how archaeologists have made some of their discoveries and what techniques are being used today to find, preserve and even rebuild some of these ancient monuments.

Although Egypt's monuments date back over 5,000 years, it has only been in the last 200 that interest in the ancient empire has grown. In 1798, Napoleon's army travelled with a group of scholars who recorded many of the monuments. Their 'Description of Egypt' helped arouse a fever of interest in Egypt. With many early tourists eager to buy antiquities as souvenirs, many Egyptians were encouraged to rob and sell their own heritage. Some of those who 'officially' dug sites were not much better. One explorer even blasted his way into a pyramid with dynamite! Since then, fortunately, digging techniques have improved and the acquisition of antiquities is subject to tighter controls.

HIEROGLYPHS

About 5,000 years ago, the Egyptians invented a form of picture writing, called hieroglyphs. Over time, their meanings were lost and they remained a mystery until the discovery in 1799 of a stone fragment near Rosetta in the Nile Delta (*above right*). It contained writings in hieroglyphs, demotic (a form of Egyptian writing) and Greek. Using this, the French scholar, Jean-François Champollion was able to work out how to read the hieroglyphs.

The first tourists were the ancient Egyptians themselves, interested in their already ancient past. But in the Late Period, when Egypt's power had declined, they started reviving old texts, art styles and cults, hoping this would restore Egypt's ancient glories. Then came Greek and Roman tourists, who ranked the pyramids at Giza (*see* pages 28-29) and the lighthouse at Alexandria (*see* pages 16-17) as two of the Seven Wonders of the World. Interest waned for many years until the late 18th century, when foreign explorers and collectors started to discover and explore the ancient sites (*below*).

MODERN EXCAVATIONS

Modern excavations involve careful, scientific research (*above*). They use the latest technology to discover and record new remains, including the use of sonar (*below*). The aim is not just to find beautiful objects but to learn everything we can about how the ancient Egyptians lived, what they did, how and why they did it and what they felt and believed.

DISCOVERING TUTANKHAMUN

The most famous discovery of ancient Egyptian remains was that of the tomb of Tutankhamun. The entrance to the tomb was uncovered in 1922 by the English archaeologist Howard Carter and, over the next few years, the tomb gave up a treasure trove of artefacts, including beds, chairs, bows and arrows and trumpets (one of which was even played some years later at the Cairo Museum). But perhaps the greatest discovery inside the tomb were the coffins of the king. Most amazing was the third coffin, which was made from 110 kg (296 lb) of solid gold!

UNDERWATER TREASURES

Excavating remains is difficult under normal conditions. But when they lie submerged on the seabed, it makes things a lot harder. Archaeologists have to cope with shifting water currents, as well as not being able to breathe without the help of special equipment. This equipment has only been developed in recent years, and with it archaeologists are retrieving remains that were once thought lost for ever. These include the remains of part of a city of the ancient world. Founded by Alexander the Great in 331 BC, Alexandria grew to become one of the greatest cities in the Mediterranean world. It declined in late Roman times, and, after the Arabs founded Cairo, Alexandria was neglected. Earthquakes caused some buildings to collapse and slip into the sea, while others simply crumbled away. Here they remained until 1994, when a team of French and Egyptian divers started bringing bits to the surface.

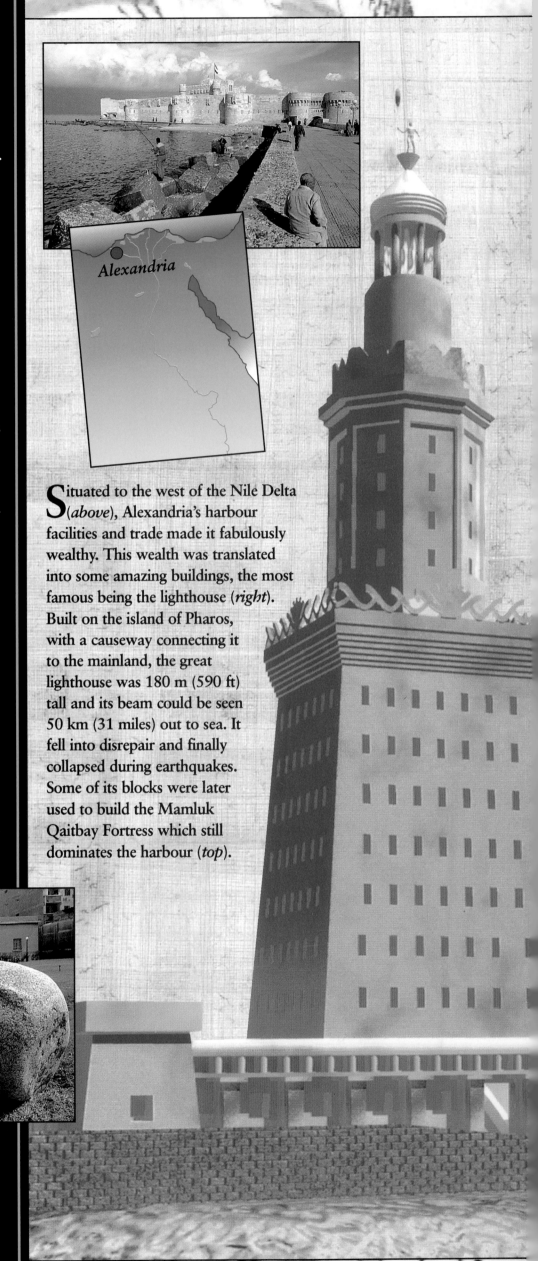

Situated to the west of the Nile Delta (*above*), Alexandria's harbour facilities and trade made it fabulously wealthy. This wealth was translated into some amazing buildings, the most famous being the lighthouse (*right*). Built on the island of Pharos, with a causeway connecting it to the mainland, the great lighthouse was 180 m (590 ft) tall and its beam could be seen 50 km (31 miles) out to sea. It fell into disrepair and finally collapsed during earthquakes. Some of its blocks were later used to build the Mamluk Qaitbay Fortress which still dominates the harbour (*top*).

Granite statue retrieved from the seabed.

CLEOPATRA

For much of the Late Period (c.712–332 BC), Egypt was under the rule of a succession of foreign kings and queens, including Nubians, Assyrians and Persians. Then came the Ptolemies who were descended from General Ptolemy, a commander in Alexander the Great's army which conquered Egypt in 332 BC. Perhaps the most famous of these was Cleopatra VII. She used her cunning to woo the Roman generals Julius Caeser and Marc Antony. In doing so she greatly improved Egypt's standing in the world. However, she also succeeded in annoying many back in Rome. In the end Rome invaded and conquered Egypt. Cleopatra committed suicide and Egypt lost its independence, falling under the direct rule of Rome.

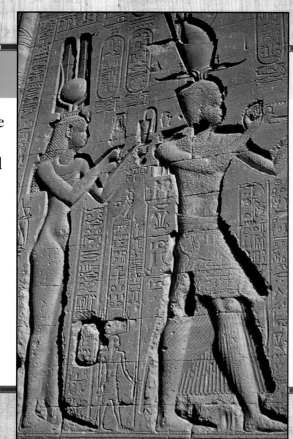

The lighthouse of Alexandria

WORKING UNDERWATER

The remains of ancient Alexandria were first discovered on the floor of the harbour in 1916. During the 1960s, Egyptian archaeologist Kamal Abu el Sadat discovered huge statues among the rubble. Things eventually came to a head when plans were announced for a concrete breakwater to sit over the area where the statues had been spotted. Archaeologists began to work quickly to retrieve as much of the ancient city as they could. During the underwater investigation of the site, divers painstakingly mapped out the remains, plotting the positions of the main pieces so that they could be brought up later (*below*). Using computers and specially designed software, the archaeologists could plot the positions of the remains to an accuracy of 10-30 cm (4-12 in). So far, some 34 large statues, including this pink granite bust (*left*), and pieces of buildings have been raised.

Diving archaeologists lifting remains from an underwater site.

SAVING HISTORY

After surviving earthquakes, floods and other natural disasters for thousands of years, Egypt's remaining monuments are now under threat from increasing human interference. In 1960, the United Nations Educational, Scientific and Cultural Organisation (UNESCO) launched a campaign to study the sites in Nubia to the south of Egypt and a province of the empire. These sites were in danger of being drowned when the Aswan Dam was built forming Lake Nasser behind it. A total of 23 temples were taken down and rebuilt elsewhere. Some even left the country! The temple of Dendut was given to the United States in gratitude for the help during the enormous project.

Other threats include vandalism (many sites are covered with graffiti, *below*) while others are simply crumbling due to the millions of tourists who walk through them year after year.

A MAMMOTH MOVE

Three thousand years ago, Ramesses II built two spectacular rock-cut temples at Abu Simbel in Nubia to honour three gods, one goddess and himself and his queen, Nefertari. Rather than leave them to drown beneath the rising waters of Lake Nasser, the temples were carved into huge blocks and moved to artificial mounds above the waters of the lake (*below*).

Another monument was the temple of Isis at Philae (*left*). Already partially drowned by an earlier dam, the temple was carefully dismantled and rebuilt on a nearby island.

Artificial mounds

Over the years, the Sphinx at Giza has suffered from the elements and humans. At one stage it was even used as an artillery target! Today, the main threat comes from the weather. Salts discovered in the mortar were eating away at the statue. Over a period of ten years the statue was repaired (*below*) and a new covering of limestone was added to protect the core. The renovated Sphinx was revealed in 1998.

BEFORE AND AFTER

After its discovery in the Valley of the Queens in 1904, the staggeringly beautiful tomb of Queen Nefertari began to deteriorate rapidly and had to be closed. Sweating visitors had made the air so damp that salt crystals emerged, pushing the paint off the walls! The Getty Conservation Institute and the Egyptian Antiquities Service embarked on the slow, delicate work of removing the salt, fixing the plaster back onto the walls and cleaning the paint (*left*). The delicate process took a total of nine years to complete, and the tomb was re-opened to the public in November 1995.

TOURISM

Every year, around three million people visit Egypt to gaze at the impressive monuments left by its ancient empire. Whilst bringing into Egypt much needed money, the sheer weight of numbers attracted to the sites can have disastrous consequences. Millions of pairs of feet can wear away paths, people brush up against fragile paintings and carvings and the breath of thousands of tourists can damage delicate remains beyond repair (*see above*). Some sites have had to be closed because of the damage which they have suffered, but rather than leave them shut permanently, archaeologists have started the painstaking process of repairing these sites to their former glory.

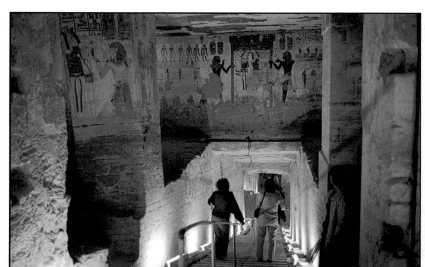

REBUILDING THE PAST

With the help of modern science, archaeologists can now learn a great deal more than their predecessors could have done, both about sites and the objects found in them. X-rays and CAT scans can look inside mummies without having to unwrap them. Planes and hot-air balloons let archaeologists get a bird's-eye view of the countryside to spot any buried buildings. Scientists can remove microscopic parts of ancient bodies and examine them to find out who was related to who (*see right*).

The advent of powerful computers has also allowed archaeologists the chance to rebuild the past. Using what they know of the shattered remnants that litter Egypt, they can recreate what monuments looked like, allowing computer-generated pyramids and temples to rise from the ground. They can even rebuild the faces of the Egyptian rulers, allowing us to gaze into the eyes of these once-powerful people.

X-rays are rays of light that we cannot see. They have so much energy that they can pass through many solid objects. Scientists can use special types of photographic film to record what these x-rays pass through and what they don't. The result is a picture of the inside of an object. In this case, the skeleton of a mummy can be seen inside a coffin (*left*).

GENE BANK

Inside every cell of our bodies is a long string-like substance which governs what we look like. It is called Deoxyribonucleic acid, or DNA (*right*). Scientists can remove DNA from a mummy and find out which family it came from by comparing it with DNA from other mummies. It has been decided to set up an ancient Egyptian DNA bank, using all the Egyptian mummies in museums across the world.

COMPUTER RECONSTRUCTIONS

If you can feed enough measurements and details into a computer, the process known as Computer Aided Design (CAD) can 'rebuild' a ruined building for you. For some 30 years, French scholars have been working at Sakkara on the ruined pyramid complex of Pepi I, a king of Dynasty VI, who reigned some 4,300 years ago. Their mass of data has been used in a CAD of the pyramid and its mortuary temple (*below*), allowing us to appreciate the original splendour of this now-ruined monument.

Buried buildings usually cannot be seen from the ground, but they become visible from the air. As this picture of the Workmen's Village (*above*) shows, the outlines of buildings are easy to spot on the desert floor of Egypt. Flying over the countryside and taking photographs has become standard practice. A hot-air balloon has been used for aerial photography recently for both the Amarna dig and the survey of the West Bank at Thebes.

Pepi I's pyramid

Mortuary temple

Queen's pyramids

A coaxial tomagraphy (CAT) scanner (*right*) is a special kind of x-ray machine. It takes slice-like images through an object without the need to open the object up and damage it. Scientists can then manipulate these 'slices' and build up three-dimensional views of the whole object.

FACE FROM THE PAST

Despite the attempts of the ancient Egyptians to preserve their dead, many corpses have deteriorated to the extent that all that is left is a skeleton. However, scientists can reconstruct the faces of these corpses using either modelling clay or computers. Scientists can recreate the muscles by examining the attachment points where they joined the bone. Finally, the thickness of the flesh can be calculated and skin can be added using the computer or clay to complete the face, letting us see the face of somebody who has been dead for thousands of years (*left*).

CHAPTER THREE
THE LOST WIFE

Egypt's monuments do more than just provide us with amazing beauty. They also tell us a great deal about how the ancient Egyptians lived. This chapter will examine how the latest discoveries have solved many mysteries about Egyptian life and, in particular, the arrangements of Egyptian royalty, including mystery wives, intermarriage and even a royal murder!

One important mystery involves the 14th-century-BC king, Akhenaten. Inscriptions from the early part of his reign show that he was besotted with his wife, Nefertiti. However, recently found evidence shows that there was a second woman in his life, referred to as "Dearly Beloved Wife, Kiya". The revelation that Kiya had a tomb in the Valley of the Kings shows that this mystery wife was very important. She may also have been the mother of Akhenaten's heir, Tutankhamun.

Inside tomb KV55, archaeologists found a beautiful coffin (*left*). However, the coffin was unable to reveal any clues as to the identity of the body it contained. The inscriptions that would have borne the name of the person inside had been deliberately hacked away. It is now thought that the coffin belonged to Kiya at one time, but archaeologists are still unsure whose body was inside when it was found.

As well as the beautiful coffin, tomb KV55 contained four special containers called canopic jars (*left*). Topped with stoppers shaped as human heads, these jars contained the internal organs of the mummy, such as the intestines and the liver. These had been removed from the body and carefully preserved.

THE MYSTERY TOMB

In 1907, a tomb in the Valley of the Kings, labelled KV55, was discovered by an American businessman Theodore Davis. He set about clearing the tomb very quickly. A little too quickly, as many of the artefacts were damaged and even destroyed in the clearance. Davis noted that during the removal of the mummy "the front teeth fell into the dust when touched". But who was in the tomb? Originally it was believed that the tomb was built for Akhenaten's mother, Queen Tiy. However, further examination of the mummy suggests that the body was that of a man, but exactly who still remains a mystery.

TUTANKHAMUN

When Akhenaten died, he was succeeded by his son, Tutankhamun, whose mother, many archaeologists believe, was Kiya. When he came to the throne, Tutankhamun was about eight years old and so had regents to rule for him. As was the custom, he married his half-sister, Ankhesenamun (*see bottom*). In all, Tutankhamun only reigned for nine years and examinations of his skeleton indicate that his life may have finished abruptly. X-rays of the skull (*below*) suggest that his death may have been a murder, caused by a blow to the back of the head!

This family tree reveals just how complex the relationships of Egyptian royal life could get. Incest and intermarriage were common. For example, Ankhesenamun probably ended up marrying her father, her half-brother and her grandfather (right).

KEY

KING   MALE CHILD   QUEEN   FEMALE CHILD

THE FEMALE KING

The reign of Akhenaten was unique. He abandoned many of the traditional ways of Egypt, adopting a new religion and building a new capital city at Amarna (*see* pages 26-27). After his reign, Egypt returned to its traditional ways, branding Akhenaten a heretic and demolishing his temples. The rubble from these ruins was then used in the foundations of other buildings. Archaeologists have been discovering these shattered remains for over 70 years. However, they have only recently begun the process of piecing them together, like an enormous jigsaw puzzle, to rebuild Akhenaten's shattered monuments. From them they have learnt a lot about his reign and have been able to answer many problems about his reign, including a new role for his favourite wife, Nefertiti (*below*).

Painted bust of Queen Nefertiti

A NEW RELIGION

After rejecting many of Egypt's traditions, Akhenaten created a new religion, around an old sun god, Aten. The most commonly used symbol for Aten was the sun disc with rays of light coming from it (*below*). However, the new religion was short lived, and after Akhenaten's death Egypt returned to its old religion, his new capital city was deserted and his temples were demolished.

One of the Aten shrines built by Akhenaten at Karnak was for Nefertiti's use alone. The focus of the shrine was a huge pillared courtyard decorated only with female figures (right). *As with many of Akhenaten's monuments, this shrine was demolished after his reign.*

After the 12th year of Akhenaten's reign, references to Nefertiti (*left*) stop. Many archaeologists believed that she had fallen out of favour. However, a recent theory based on inscriptions found on the demolished temples indicates that Akhenaten may have made her his co-ruler. She effectively became a king, ruling by his side for the rest of his reign. She may also have outlived him. If so, she died early in Tutankhamun's reign.

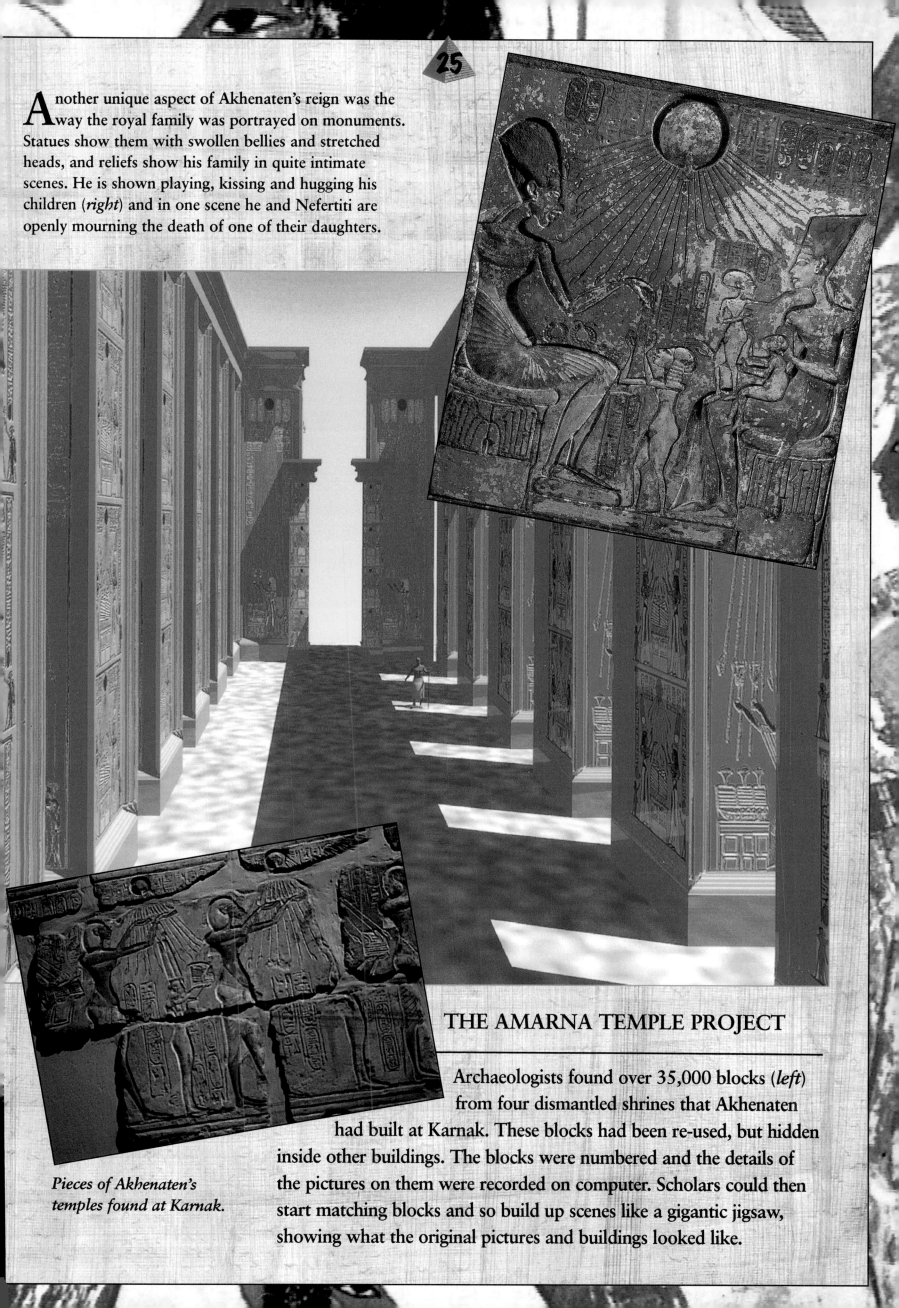

Another unique aspect of Akhenaten's reign was the way the royal family was portrayed on monuments. Statues show them with swollen bellies and stretched heads, and reliefs show his family in quite intimate scenes. He is shown playing, kissing and hugging his children (*right*) and in one scene he and Nefertiti are openly mourning the death of one of their daughters.

THE AMARNA TEMPLE PROJECT

Archaeologists found over 35,000 blocks (*left*) from four dismantled shrines that Akhenaten had built at Karnak. These blocks had been re-used, but hidden inside other buildings. The blocks were numbered and the details of the pictures on them were recorded on computer. Scholars could then start matching blocks and so build up scenes like a gigantic jigsaw, showing what the original pictures and buildings looked like.

Pieces of Akhenaten's temples found at Karnak.

Building the Pyramids

The pyramids at Giza (*see bottom*) have attracted so much study and excavation, you would think there was nothing left to find. Over the last ten years, however, archaeologists have made a variety of important new discoveries. These have included a second funeral boat, paved roads linking the pyramids to quarries, a town for priests and officials who served the pyramid and a cemetery for dead workers. They have also discovered housing for the twenty to thirty thousand workers that lived nearby at any one time, as well as buildings dedicated to feeding, clothing and looking after their needs, including a bakery and a place where fish were dried and stored for meals. All of these discoveries have given scholars a peek into the organisation behind one of the largest building projects ever undertaken.

EARTHQUAKE!

This picture highlights one of the problems faced by Egypt's monuments. Taken by an Austrian tourist in 1992, it shows stones, dust and debris tumbling down the side of the step pyramid at Sakkara. The dust and debris were dislodged by an earthquake.

Many other monuments have been completely destroyed by earthquakes and landslides, including Tuthmosis III's temple (*see* page 9).

THE WORKFORCE

The pyramids were NOT built by slaves. There was a permanent force of skilled stone-masons, plus an army of labourers who hauled the stones. As money had not yet been invented, taxes were paid in goods and labour. The stone-haulers were ordinary peasants, paying their labour-tax to the king. During their 3-month stint, the king fed, clothed and housed them. The men were divided into gangs. A gang would load a stone block on to a sledge, then haul it up a ramp into place (*right*).

Giza

The pyramid complex at Giza

1 Menkhare's pyramid, 2 Khafre's pyramid,
3 Khufu's pyramid, 4 Khafre's workshops,
5 Khufu's quarry, 6 Menkhare's quarry,
7 Khentkawe's town, 8 Bakery site,
9 Possible ramp site and Khafre's quarry,
10 Mastaba tombs.

In the late 1980s, a cemetery was uncovered for men who worked on the pyramids (*below*). Many of the skeletons had broken bones, but they were well mended as doctors were on site to help sick workmen. The skeletons also show heavy wear and tear on joints and backs, as well as bony growths due to heavy labour.

In 1995, a team of scientists set about trying to recreate the building of the pyramids using the same methods employed by the ancient Egyptians. Although on a much smaller scale than the great pyramids at Giza, they showed that teams of ten to twenty men could haul the massive stones used in the pyramids' construction up an earth ramp (*above*).

SPY CAMERA

In 1954, two graves were discovered next to Khufu's pyramid. They contained the remains of boats that were to carry the king in the afterlife. One of these graves was opened and the boat inside was rebuilt and today stands in a museum next to the pyramid. The other grave was left untouched until 1987. Archaeologists devised a camera with an air-lock which could enter the grave without disturbing the air inside the grave (*right*). Unfortunately the grave had already been damaged and was no longer air-tight, but the method will prove invaluable to investigate newly found tombs.

Glossary & TIMELINE

Abydos
Egyptian city that was sacred to Osiris, the god of the dead. Archaeologists believe it to be the resting place of the earliest Egyptian kings.

Alexandria
City on the Mediterranean coast, founded by Alexander the Great, the Macedonian king who conquered Egypt. The city contained an impressive library and a huge lighthouse which was one of the Seven Wonders of the Ancient World.

Amarna
The site of the city of Akhetaten, one of the ancient capitals of Egypt founded by the pharaoh Akhenaten.

Archaeologist
A person who uncovers and studies historical remains.

Canopic jars
Small jars that were used to hold the intestines of a dead body after they had been removed during mummification.

Hieroglyphs
A form of ancient Egyptian writing which uses small pictures instead of letters.

Hyksos
A people of unknown origin who settled in the Nile Delta and ruled Egypt from their capital Avaris. Their name comes from two ancient Egyptian words meaning 'rulers of foreign hill countries.'

Mastaba
From the Arabic for 'bench', mastabas are rectangular buildings which cover the tombs of some of Egypt's earliest kings and nobles.

Memphis
The capital of Egypt for almost 400 years, it lies on the west bank of the Nile just south of the modern-day capital, Cairo.

1960 Temples at Abu Simbel dismantled and moved.

1799 Rosetta Stone is discovered.

Mummy
The preserved remains of a dead person. Egyptian mummies were either preserved naturally by the drying-out effects of the sand, or artificially by using natron, a salt which was used as a drying agent during the process of mummification.

1998 Renovation of the Sphinx completed.

1954 Boat is discovered next to the pyramids at Giza.

1922 Howard Carter discovers the tomb of Tutankhamun.

Nile
The river which flows through Egypt. Its waters were, and still are, vital to Egypt, watering the crops along its banks.

Osiris
The ancient Egyptian god and king of the Dead.

Pharaoh
A title used by the rulers of Egypt from the Amarna period onwards. It comes from the name for a royal palace, the 'per-aa', or Great House.

Regent
A person who effectively rules for the monarch. This is because the monarch is too young to rule in person. In ancient Egypt, for example, Hatshepsut acted as regent for the young King Tuthmosis III.

Sakkara
Found on the edge of the desert, Sakkara was an important site as it was used as a cemetery throughout the period of ancient Egypt.

Stela
An inscribed stone slab. Those placed in or near tombs act as memorials to the dead and pray for food and drink in the next world.

Temple
A building constructed for the worship of a god or goddess.

Tomb
A room or building constructed to hold the body of a dead person. The Egyptians built underground tombs, tombs cut into cliffs and huge pyramids to hold the bodies of their rulers and nobles.

UNESCO
The United Nations Educational, Scientific and Cultural Organisation. This organisation was responsible for the relocation of 23 temples away from the rising waters of Lake Nasser.

Valley of the Kings
Found on the West Bank of the Nile, opposite the modern town of Luxor, this valley contains the bodies of the kings from the New Kingdom, as well as some of their families and associates.

Valley of the Queens
Found next to the Valley of the Kings, this valley was used for the burial of queens and royal children from the 19th and 20th Dynasties.

THE PHARAOH'S MUMMY

THE WRAPPING

Once the internal organs had been removed and the corpse preserved using oils and a salt called natron, the body of the mummy was wrapped tightly

E
AOH'S
MY

FUNERARY AMULETS

Among the bandages of the mummy, priests would place special carved objects called amulets (above). These would give magical protection to the wearer when he or she passed into the next world.

amulet

: great care in

heir dead, ensuring that they

s comfortably as

mmies were placed in a

nese were usually painted to

se for an important person,

of solid gold (*above*). The

coffins deep inside tombs.

X RAY
Today, scientists
can use modern
technology to study
mummies without
damaging them. X rays
are able to pass through
many solid objects and
can be recorded on
special film to form a
picture (above).

in bandages (above). This picture of an ancient Egyptian mummy (below) shows how successful they became at preserving their dead.

The ancient Egyptians took preserving the bodies of could enjoy the afterlife possible. The specially preserved mu number of coffins, or sarcophagi. T look like the dead person, while tho such as a king, were even made out coffins were then lowered into ston